RECREATION
in History

PICTURE HISTORY

PICTURE HISTORY

RECREATION
IN HISTORY

Alan Blackwood

First published in 1984 by
Wayland (Publishers) Limited
49 Lansdowne Place, Hove
East Sussex BN3 1HF, England

© Copyright 1984 Wayland (Publishers) Ltd

ISBN 0 85078 395 X

Series design by Behram Kapadia

Phototypeset by Kalligraphics Ltd, Redhill, Surrey
Printed in Italy by G. Canale & C.S.p.A., Turin
Bound in the U.K. by The Pitman Press, Bath

Contents

Introduction

Recreation is play or relaxation. It nearly always involves participation – sharing in an event, an occasion, whether as contestant, performer or spectator. At its best, it also means 're-creating' our time, adding to our experience of being alive.

Big Business

Today, when most of us have the time and money to follow whatever sport, art or other entertainment attracts us, recreation is big business. The great spectator sports, like football and motor racing, and the performing arts of theatre, opera, cinema and television, deal in huge sums of money. So recreation is important not only to us individually, but to the community and the economy.

In times past, when most people had to work hard just to stay alive, recreation may not have commanded so much money and attention. But sports, games and pastimes, music, dancing and theatre, have been around for as long as men and women have wanted to enjoy themselves. And because of their rich variety, these recreational activities have probably reflected more of history as a whole than any other single branch of human affairs.

The pageants and tournaments of the Middle Ages, for example, grew directly out of the art of war as it was waged in those far-off days. The story of chess tells us even more about warfare and conquest over the last two and half thousand years.

The beginnings of the circus take us right back to the days when Rome was capital of the world's mightiest empire. Fairgrounds first sprang up round churches at the time of the great medieval religious feasts and festivals.

Fashions and Manners

Sports, art and entertainments have often reflected fashions and manners too. Ballet at the huge palaces and gardens of Versailles in the days of the French King Louis XIV included gorgeous displays of fashion. And in Victorian England, when it was considered the right and proper thing to do, gentlemen played cricket in top hats.

Down the ages, all this has inspired a kaleidoscope of illustration: beautiful 'illuminated' scenes from priceless old manuscripts; masterpieces of painting and engraving; bright and breezy sporting prints; lively drawings of such old favourites as Punch and Judy; colourful circus posters; and, moving on to the present, stunning action photos of big moments in sport, pop stars on stage, and the excitement of such unique events as the Last Night of the Proms.

So the story of recreation is a marvellous education too, as this book shows.

N celle saisoyet
entretant que les
treuces se tenoi
ent en france et
en angleterre pur mer et par terre

que le puis Sauuerayne en recep
uoit les plaintes en venoient a
puris eut conseil le roy de fran
ce denoyer deuers le roy dangle
terre et lui escripze et sumsier

Medieval Tournaments

Tournaments were very popular in the Middle Ages. They were tests of horsemanship and soldierly skills, at a time when knights-at-arms were some of the most important people in the land.

Jousting

In this picture, two mounted knights are riding up to each other on either side of a fence. Each is aiming to unseat the other by a stroke from his lance. It was a skilful exercise, as a knight had to hold his long, heavy lance at just the right angle to strike his opponent effectively. Such contests were called jousting.

Not all tournaments were as gentlemanly as this one. Sometimes two groups of heavily armed knights just lined up and charged at each other, as they might in a real battle. It was not unusual for many of them to be killed or seriously hurt.

Only rich people could afford to take part in tournaments. They had to pay for their horses and suits of armour, which would be like running a racing car today. They also had to pay their squires – the lads who fed and groomed the horses and polished up all the expensive armour. And if they were organizing the tournament, they would be expected to entertain the other lords and ladies who attended.

We can see from all the pageantry in this picture that the people taking part belong to rich and noble families. The knight on the right-hand side has an elaborate emblem of his family crest fixed to his helmet. Other contestants are holding shields which bear their family coat of arms. Notice too that coats of arms have been slung round the tops of the tents.

Coats of Arms

Each noble family in medieval times had its own proud coat of arms. This might include the image of an animal, such as a lion or a boar, the design of a flower or a leaf, or be composed of white or dark stripes and dots on coloured backgrounds. Such symbols displayed on shields and banners were very useful to feudal lords, when they wanted to lead their soldiers into battle.

In this picture, a few lords and ladies are watching the jousting from the decorated stand in the background. In fact, thousands of people sometimes turned up at tournaments.

The picture itself comes from an illuminated manuscript dating from about 1350. In the centuries before printing was invented, all books had to be written by hand. They were 'illuminated' with the kind of beautifully decorated initial letter shown here, and with pictures such as this.

templū

tabula moyfi

levita

VOGA

ne hocꝰ Auph vernmm · ꝑ ferta ſmutitoꝵꝵ ·

Early Musical Instruments

This illustration is also taken from an illuminated manuscript. It shows a group of musicians, and dates from around 1425. Going from left to right, the slightly curved wind instruments are cornetts, which were blown like a brass instrument but had holes in the side of the tube for playing different notes, like a woodwind instrument. Then there is someone playing a lute (a plucked, stringed instrument) and another playing a fiddle or *viele* (a bowed, stringed instrument). In the lower right-hand corner is a man with a triangle (a percussion instrument), and right at the back is a harpist (the harp being another plucked, stringed instrument).

Notice that there is a second man with a harp over on the left of the picture, standing outside the building. Perhaps he's not wanted by the others, which is why he looks rather cross!

Turning Point in Music

There were many other musical instruments of the period besides those featured here. Among wind instruments, there were some with such quaint names as shawm, pommer, crumhorn and rackett. Percussion instruments included kettledrums; tabors, a small drum slung round the neck by a chord; cymbals; and sets of small bells or 'chimes' which were hit with a hammer.

There were plucked, stringed instruments mounted on little sounding boards, which were called dulcimers and psalteries.

In fact, the date of this picture marks a turning point in European music. Before this time – back in the Middle Ages – most music was sung, either by choirs in church, or by minstrels, though in both cases instruments were often used to accompany the singing. From about the year 1400 – that is, from about the beginning of the Renaissance period – there was a tremendous growth in purely instrumental music, due to improvements in the instruments themselves, and to the fact that some people had more money and leisure time.

Collections

It became fashionable to learn to play an instrument. Ladies played small portable or 'portative' wind organs, also some of the first stringed, keyboard instruments, such as virginals (which may have been named after Elizabeth I, 'the Virgin Queen'). Gentlemen liked to build up collections or 'consorts' of the same kind of instrument made to different sizes (so playing different ranges of pitched notes). The bowed, stringed instruments called viols, and also the flute-like recorders were very popular in this respect.

Court Jesters

In the plays of Shakespeare there is often a character called The Fool, who is attached to the court of some monarch or nobleman. Originally, such people really were fools – simpletons who were just there to be laughed at. But well before Shakespeare's time, the court fool had changed into a jester – a genuine comic, clever and quick-witted. Such people sometimes had a club-foot, hunchback, or other physical deformity, which made them unfit for work or war.

Risky Position

The court jester shown here is taken from an illuminated manuscript of the fifteenth century. He has all the jester's trappings: the cap or cowl with ass's ears, little jingling bells attached to his multi-coloured tunic, and the mock sceptre or bauble with its own jester's head sticking its tongue out. Some baubles were fitted instead with a bladder, filled with air or dried peas, that the jester used for hitting people over the head.

Jesters were often in a powerful position at court. They enjoyed the confidence of the king or queen, and could slip in a word for or against other people. On the other hand, it could be a risky business. If a jester didn't amuse the court enough, he would soon be fired. If his jokes gave offence, he might easily be in for a whipping, or possibly even lose his head.

As well as being comics, court jesters were often excellent musicians. They composed and sang songs, accompanying themselves on such instruments as a harp or a lute, or played and danced to the shawm or recorder. In this respect there is a strong link between them and the poet-musicians who also figured largely in medieval entertainment at court.

The most celebrated of these poet-musicians were the troubadours of southern France. In fact, the name 'troubadour' comes from the old Provençal word *trobar*, meaning 'to find', in the sense of inventing poems and melodies. The court of Queen Eleanor of Aquitaine in the twelfth century was the most famous meeting place for troubadours. One of her sons was Richard the Lionheart, and he was a troubadour as well as a crusader knight and king of England.

German Troubadours

In Germany, minstrels similar to the troubadours were called *minnesingers*, meaning 'singers of love'. Like the troubadours, the *minnesingers* sometimes held poetry and song contests among themselves. The Welsh eisteddfods continue such a tradition to this very day.

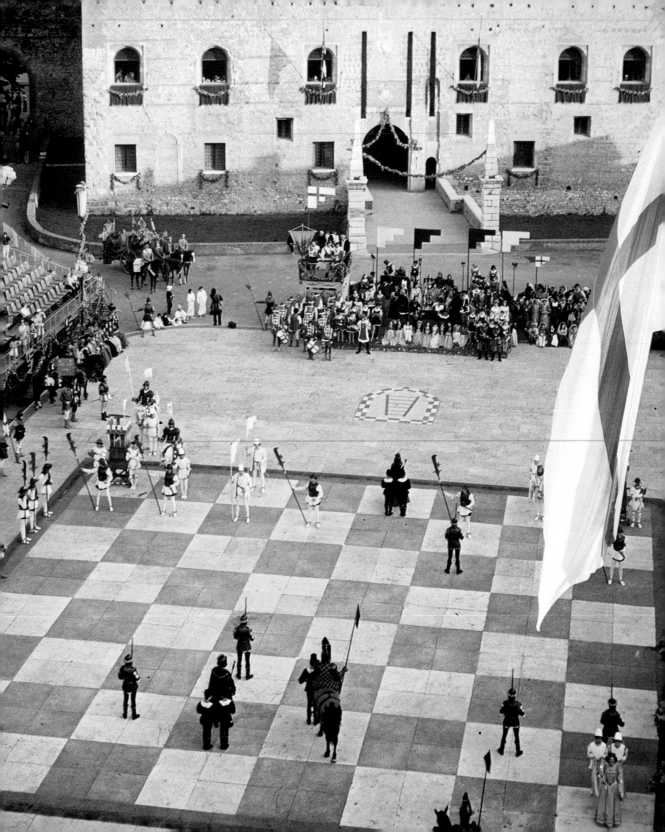

Chess

Every other year, in September, a colourful ceremony takes place in the small Italian town of Marostica. A game of chess is played in the town square, with people dressed up as the pieces.

The origin of this unique event lies back in the fifteenth century, when there were two rival suitors for the hand in marriage of the local lord's daughter. Instead of fighting a duel, the suitors agreed to settle their claim by a game of chess played in the presence of the whole town. This is the game that is re-enacted today by the good folk of the district. There they stand, as our picture shows, in their gorgeous costumes, upon a giant chess-board, while a herald calls out the moves from a nearby tower.

From India to Europe

Such an occasion highlights the fascinating story of chess. It started in northern India, about 400 BC. There it was called *chaturanga*, and was based on the traditional Indian army formation, which consisted of a mass of foot soldiers supported by cavalry, chariots (or armed boats) and elephants. Alexander the Great may have learnt this early form of the game when he marched into north-west India in 326 BC.

The Persians next took up chess. Their word for the piece called the king was *shah*, from which we get our word 'chess'. The object of the game – to place your opponent's king in a position where he cannot avoid capture – they called *shahmat*, meaning 'the king is helpless'. From this comes our term 'checkmate'.

The Royal Game

The Persian Empire was conquered by the armies of the new religion of Islam during the seventh century AD; and as the forces of Islam swept across North Africa into Spain, so the game of chess went with them. Soon it was being played everywhere in Europe, from Moorish Spain to the northern lands of Scandinavia and Iceland. By other routes, it spread to China and the Far East.

Chess became known as the 'royal game'. King Canute, the Mongol warlord Tamerlane, Tsar Ivan the Terrible and Catherine the Great of Russia, Louis XIII of France, Charles I of England, were all keen chess players. Some of the first books ever printed, by William Caxton and others, were about how to play chess.

Great chess players (grand masters) have come from all over the world. There have been François Philidor of France, Paul Morphy of the United States, José Capablanca of Cuba, and Alexander Alekhine of Russia.

Dancing

This picture of morris dancers was painted about 1620. Nobody is sure how morris dancing got its name. One theory is that it comes from the word 'Morisco', describing a very old kind of folk dance from Moorish Spain. Whatever the explanation, morris dancing itself goes back many centuries, to pagan times, when people performed strange rites and ceremonies to mark such times of the year as spring and harvest tide.

They sometimes dressed up as animals, perhaps as part of a ritual to do with hunting. Notice that one of the dancers here is fitted out with a kind of hobby horse. Another, however, is going round with a collecting plate or spoon, a sure sign that by the seventeenth century such dancing was only meant to amuse.

Folk Dancing

English morris dancing is a form of folk art. 'Folk' means 'of the people', and describes any kind of music, dancing or other activity created by a whole race or community. No one person sits down and composes a folk song or works out the steps of a folk dance. Such tunes and dances gradually take shape and go on changing all the time. Nearly every country or race has its own heritage of folk dances. In Scotland there are dances called reels and strathspeys. Russia and other Slavic lands have such dances as the dumka, which is alternately slow and sad, then wild and fast. Southern Spain is the home of the dramatic flamenco singing and dancing.

At the time of our picture, dancing was also very popular with the nobility. They usually borrowed tunes and dance steps from the humble 'folk', turning them into more graceful 'measures' and giving them elegant names such as pavane and galliard. Henry VIII (before he grew too fat), his daughter Elizabeth I, and Charles I, all loved this kind of dancing, which took a lot of practice to do well.

Ballet

Courtly dancing reached its height with the French King Louis XIV, who built the great palace of Versailles, near Paris. Louis and his courtiers planned and arranged such elaborate dances that they gave rise to the art form we now call ballet. Because ballet, as we know it, started with Louis XIV and his court, most of the terms used – *corps de ballet* (main group of dancers), *pas de deux* (dance for two people), and so on – are in French.

In the nineteenth century a type of Austrian folk dance called the *ländler* gave rise to the waltz. This proved to be the most popular dance of all time.

Blood Sports

In the long history of blood sports, one of the most widespread and popular has been cockfighting. It probably began in China, reaching Europe about the fifth century BC, when both the Greeks and the Romans enjoyed it.

Gamecocks were specially bred and trained for the sport. They had their skins and muscles toughened by massage, their feathers trimmed and the combs over their heads cut, to make them sleek and to reduce those parts of the body an opponent could attack. Like boxers, they were matched against each other by weight, and sometimes they had sharp metal spurs tied to their legs. They attacked each other with claws and beaks, and contests might end in the death of one of them, or when one or other simply backed off.

Gambling

This engraving of a cockpit was made by William Hogarth, an English artist with a genius for observing the vices of mankind, and for portraying scenes with great attention to detail. We know much of what life was like in eighteenth-century London, thanks to him.

The first thing we can see from this picture is that a lot of gambling is going on. There's somebody over on the left of the pit placing a bet with a single coin. In the centre is a much richer gentleman, to judge by his smart clothes and the banknotes he is scattering about. Someone, by the looks of it, is just about to pocket one of them for himself. Also down by the ringside is a bookmaker, indicated by Hogarth by the word 'bets' written (upside-down) on his notebook. The man next to him has other gamecocks in a bag, and may be the referee.

Snuff

Leaning over the cockpit wall is a man taking snuff – powdered tobacco that was sniffed up the nose. Several others are also indulging in the habit, one of them sneezing his head off. There's a deaf old fellow with his ear trumpet, and someone whose wig is falling off in all the excitement. Most men wore wigs in the eighteenth century. Notice that down in the right-hand corner of the picture Hogarth has etched in the shape of a gallows. That's probably where he thought some of his characters would end up!

Various forms of hunting are, of course, the best-known blood sports today. Originally, hunting was not really sport at all, but a part of the vital job of obtaining food. By the Middle Ages, though, hunting on horseback, with packs of hounds, was a favourite pastime of the nobility.

Fairs

Here is another picture by Hogarth, this time a painting. The scene is a fairground at Southwark, on London's South Bank, in 1733.

Our word 'fair' comes from the Latin *feriae*, meaning 'feast' or 'festival', and that is exactly how many fairs started. In the Middle Ages, religious feasts and festivals were also public holidays, attracting to the towns and cities strolling players, jugglers, acrobats, clowns and jesters, fortune-tellers and mountebanks (quack doctors) from miles around. So the church festivals became 'fairs'; and it is interesting to note that some fairs still take place on the old religious feast days, like Michaelmas.

Market Fairs

There were also the great medieval market 'fairs', where merchants gathered to exchange their goods. They too became a place of fun and jollity, when all the trading had been done. The Nottingham Goose Fair started as a market for poultry and game.

By the time of Hogarth's painting, 'all the fun of the fair' seems to have taken over from both religion and commerce. The church itself is almost lost behind platforms and hoardings. Theatrical entertainments are much in evidence. In the foreground a troupe of players are announcing themselves with pipe and drum; while a balcony on the right has just collapsed, sending more costumed figures tumbling on top of a man running a game of dice.

Actors and Acrobats

In the centre of the picture another troupe have a painted board advertising a spectacle called 'The Siege of Troy'. If you look closely at the board you can just make out the figures of Greek soldiers emerging from the opened-up side of the large white model horse. Next to them are more placards advertising a Punch and Judy show, a performance of which is taking place on the extreme left of the balcony (see also page 33). Other interesting features to note in the picture are the tightrope walker and acrobat (now a more familiar sight in the circus ring) and, down in the right-hand corner, a man playing the bagpipes.

Fairs changed again during the nineteenth century due to the Industrial Revolution. Steam engines were used to power big revolving roundabouts or carousels. These made a splendid sight with all their gaudily painted woodwork, mirrors and polished brass, plus the steam organs, or calliopes, that included mechanical figures clashing cymbals and beating drums. They were also fine pieces of engineering, judged by the standards of their time.

Grand Tours

In many parts of Europe, important days in the church year have been public holidays also. This is Ascension Day in Venice, painted by Giovanni Canale, or Canaletto, about the year 1750. Just arriving at the Doge's Palace on the Grand Canal is the magnificent barge of the Doge himself (the governors of Venice during the centuries when it was a rich and independent city-state were called Doges). Surrounding the barge are gondolas, full of people out to have a good time.

Birth of Tourism

Canaletto painted hundreds of scenes or views of Venice. They are rather like high-class picture postcards; and indeed he produced them mainly to sell to visitors to the city. For Canaletto lived during the eighteenth century, which saw the birth of what we now call tourism. It was given a much loftier name in those days. It was called going on a Grand Tour.

The Grand Tour was especially popular with the British. Britain at that time was gaining a large empire. But while British merchants and bankers might make their money from trade with China, India or the American colonies, they recognized that the best art, music, wines and foods still came from other parts of Europe. So with their money they went on a Grand Tour of Europe, a once-in-a-lifetime adventure that sometimes took them away from home for two or three years.

In some ways, people going on a Grand Tour were much like tourists today. They had phrase books and guide books; and instead of taking photographs, they loved to make sketches or little water-colour paintings of the famous sights. In other ways, things were very different. Tourists trundled and bumped along muddy or dusty roads in horse-drawn coaches, taking days or weeks to get from one city to the next. To get across the Alps they probably had to go by pack-mule. Some roads were notorious for bandits. In the Mediterranean, there were pirates. The prudent tourist carried arms, and a well-stocked medicine chest.

Italy

Paris, Amsterdam, the Rhine Valley, Austria, and Switzerland were all places to visit. Italy, though, was the favourite destination. Many tourists headed for Florence, centre of Renaissance art. Others went on to Rome, to marvel at the antiquities, or to Naples, to admire the Bay and wonder at the smoking form of Vesuvius. But the most popular of all was Venice, with its palaces and churches, and its canals.

Theatre

Our picture shows the interior of London's Covent Garden theatre in 1804. The Greeks enjoyed going to the theatre two thousand years before this time. Thanks to long, hot summers, their theatres were in the open air, with semi-circular rows of stone seats looking down on to a circular stone stage.

Greek playwrights, such as Aristophanes and Sophocles, created the two basic kinds of drama – comedy and tragedy. But the way they wrote and presented their plays was quite different from the kind of theatre we are used to. The actors usually wore masks, and there was a small group of other actors, called the 'chorus', who spoke or chanted a kind of running commentary upon the course of the action.

William Shakespeare

In the Middle Ages there were Miracle and Morality Plays, performed during religious festivals and holidays. They presented stories from the Bible.

The most famous plays ever written are those by William Shakespeare. He began writing at the end of the period of European history called the Renaissance, which was a time of great discovery, in the sciences and in exploration, and a time also of great new ideas in art and literature. Shakespeare portrayed the characters in his plays as real people, in a way not done before.

Shakespeare himself belonged to a theatrical company, and almost certainly acted in some of his own plays. One of the places these were staged was at the Globe theatre in London. The Globe had a stage raised above the level of the ground floor, which was called the pit. The audience stood in the pit. Other members of the audience sat in small galleries above and around it.

Proscenium Arch

The Covent Garden theatre pictured here dates from about two hundred years after the time of Shakespeare and the Globe. The stage has a much more familiar look to it. It is built with what is called a proscenium arch – a structure from which the curtain rises and falls. The scenery looks most realistic. A famous English actor and theatre manager, David Garrick, had been the first to use much more elaborate scenery and lighting effects. People came from all over Europe to admire productions at his Drury Lane theatre (just down the road from Covent Garden).

Notice, though, that the audience down in the pit are still standing. They also appear to be as much interested in each other as in the performance. Theatres and opera houses were favourite meeting places in those days.

Horse-Racing

This artist's impression of The Derby – the world's most famous horse-race – comes from the *Illustrated London News* of 1846. Some of the spectators in the grand stand appear to have their binoculars already trained on the winning post ahead of the horses. The gentleman in the middle foreground, with hand raised nervously to lips, looks unhappy with the way the race is going!

See how the crowd in the distance is pouring on to the track behind the horses. Over on the far right of the picture, among the tents and marquees, there seems to be another race going on. Notice how the horses are all portrayed with their legs stretched full out. Galloping horses were always depicted this way, until photographs showed that they never actually run like that.

The Sport of Kings

Horse-racing – 'The Sport of Kings' – has an ancient history. The writing on a clay tablet found in Asia Minor (north-west Turkey), and dating back to 1400 BC, has been deciphered as a set of rules about horse-racing. In our own era, the sport goes back to about the time of Henry I (1086–1135), who pioneered the cross-breeding of small, swift Arab steeds with the larger, tougher English breeds. The first true race track was opened at Smithfield, London, in 1174.

Horse-racing today is organized under two main headings. There is flat racing, which takes place over level grass or turf tracks (horse-racing is also known as 'The Turf'); and there is steeplechasing, which involves jumping over fences, hedges and other obstacles.

The Derby is the most celebrated of all flat races. It takes place at Epsom racecourse, and was started in 1780. The story goes that the then Earl of Derby and a friend named Sir Charles Bunbury decided on whose name should be given to the race by the toss of a coin. If the story is true, then we might now be talking of 'The Bunbury' instead!

The Grand National

The most famous steeplechase is the Grand National, founded in 1837 and run for many years at Aintree racecourse, near Liverpool. Over the years, a number of horses and jockeys have been badly injured or killed in this race.

The United States also has some notable horse-racing tracks and events, including the Kentucky Derby, founded in 1875. It is also the home of 'harness racing'. Here, the jockeys ride on small, light-weight, two-wheeled vehicles attached to the animal by shafts. Such racing is an interesting step back in time towards those breath-taking chariot races of ancient Greece and Rome.

Zoos

Everybody loves going to the zoo, to watch the chimpanzees and penguins, or feed buns to the elephants. But zoos are also places of much deeper interest. The word 'zoo' is short for zoology or zoological – the scientific study of animal life (all life, really, from ants to human beings).

Court Menageries

Zoological gardens, to give them their full name, have a long history. A Chinese emperor created a 'Park of Intelligence' as long ago as 1150 BC. This apparently included many varieties, or species, of mammal, bird, reptile and fish. The pharaohs of ancient Egypt, and the kings of Babylon and Assyria, also liked to keep wild animals, though this was probably more to attract attention to themselves than to study animal life.

In the Middle Ages and Renaissance times, rare creatures from Africa and India, such as lions, leopards, peacocks, and monkeys too, were sometimes exchanged between kings and queens as extravagant birthday or wedding presents. At the wedding feast for Philip the Good of Burgundy and Isabella of Portugal in 1430, an elephant was led into the banqueting hall, decorated in silk and bearing a large model castle on its back. Court menageries were the wonders of the age. Across the seas, in Mexico the Aztec King Montezuma also had a marvellous menagerie of animals brought to him from different parts of the Americas.

True zoological gardens only date from the nineteenth century. The world-famous London Zoo was founded in 1829 – which is about the date of this charming picture. It is presented as a guided tour to the zoo. We can see some birds in an aviary, a pair of ostriches, lions, a wolf (hopefully in a separate cage), bears, elephants, monkeys, and what look like a pair of beavers or otters.

Most of the creatures are shown in cages. Modern zoos are getting rid of these as fast as they can, so that the animals can appear much more at home and less like prisoners. Safari parks are the best places for seeing animals living as closely as possible to the way they would in the wild.

Jigsaw Puzzle

An interesting thing to note about our picture is that it is in the form of a jigsaw puzzle. As far as we know, the jigsaw puzzle was invented in 1762 by an English printer named John Spilsburg. His first puzzle was a black-and-white print of a map glued to a wooden board and cut into a few simple shapes. He called it a 'dissected map', and intended it to help children learn geography.

31

Punch and Judy

'Oh dear, oh dear!' squawks Mr Punch as his wife Judy beats him with a stick. Note in this picture the jester's bauble included in the coat of arms above the stage, which is interesting to compare with the bauble in the picture on page 14. Seventy years ago, Punch and Judy shows were a common sight in British towns and cities, and at the seaside. They are rarer today, but children still love them.

Puppet Theatre

Punch and Judy and all the other characters involved belong to the fascinating world of puppet theatre. In the Far East puppets are mostly in the form of cut-out figures operated by rods from the side of the stage. Italy is the traditional home of marionettes which are manipulated by strings from above the stage. The little character named Pinocchio is a famous example of a marionette. Punch and Judy are glove puppets, with heads and hands that fit over the showman's own hands and are animated from below the stage.

Glove puppet shows were once popular all over Europe. One of the characters that regularly appeared in them was a clown named Pulcinella. He was borrowed from a special kind of live theatre that began in Italy, called *Commedia dell' Arte*, or 'Professional Theatre' (see also page 37). His name changed from country to country. In France, he was Polichinelle. In England, he was named Punchinello, and finally plain Mr Punch.

Wicked Mr Punch!

For some time, Mr Punch appeared in a wide variety of puppet plays. By about 1800, though, he began to settle into the role that was to become so familiar to generations of British children. In this part, Mr Punch has a wife, originally named Joan, and then Judy. Judy leaves him at home to mind the baby. The baby starts crying, so Mr Punch throws her out of the window. Judy returns and starts to beat him. In reply, he beats her to death.

Other characters, including a doctor and a policeman, also take a beating from Mr Punch. Then the hangman comes for him, but the crafty fellow gets the hangman to put his own head into the noose. At last the Devil arrives to cart Mr Punch off to Hell; but after a terrific fight, Mr Punch beats the Devil as well.

By tradition, the showman speaks the parts in a pinched, high-pitched voice that he produces with the aid of a small whistle-like object called a swazzle or squeaker. Many showmen also used to have a live dog called Toby, trained to sit by the booth and then collect money in a little bag at the end of the performance.

LEG HALF VOLLEY.

Cricket

The batsman in this cricketing print of 1845 has no leg pads or gloves, and appears to be wearing casual shoes instead of boots. Altogether he cuts a jolly figure. He might almost be dancing a sailor's hornpipe if it weren't for the bat.

By the time of this picture, cricket already had a long history. A document dated 1598 – ten years after the Spanish Armada – tells of somebody 'playing at cricket'. Apparently the ball was rolled along the ground and struck at by a kind of bat rather like a hockey stick. It may have been modelled on a traditional shepherd's crook. Some people suggest that the actual name of 'cricket' comes from the word 'crook'.

The Ashes

It was during the eighteenth century that cricket really got going. One of the first true cricket clubs was formed about the year 1750, in the Hampshire village of Hambledon. Another early club was the White Conduit Club at Islington in London. It moved to a new ground in Marylebone in 1787, renaming itself the Marylebone Cricket Club, or the MCC. In 1814 the MCC played its first match on its present ground, Lord's, which is named after Thomas Lord who handled the purchase of the land. Ever since, the MCC and Lord's cricket ground have been recognized as the headquarters of the game.

Cricket was being played in Australia by 1850, and the first-ever test match between an English and an Australian side was played in Melbourne in 1877. This brings us to the story of The Ashes, the great cricketing trophy. Australia beat England for the first time at London's other famous cricket ground, The Oval, in 1882. A newspaper announced this defeat with a notice joking about the death and cremation of English cricket, adding that the ashes would be shipped to Australia.

That same winter England won a test match series in Australia, at the end of which part of a set of stumps was burnt and some real ashes placed in an urn. This is The Ashes. It has long been kept at Lord's, no matter whether it is England or Australia that has actually gained the trophy.

Over-Arm Bowling

Women have played cricket as well. Indeed, they had a hand in the big change from under-arm to over-arm bowling that took place during the nineteenth century. Playing in the wide crinoline petticoats of the period, they could not easily bowl under-arm, so took to pitching the ball round the body or over the head.

Pantomime

The lower picture on the left is a scene from a Victorian pantomime of 1851. The character in the centre of the stage is Oliver Cromwell, while the one peering anxiously down from the tree is meant to be Charles I. The title of the piece is 'Oliver Cromwell, or Harlequin Charley over the Water and the Maid of Patty's Mill'. Pantomimes like this don't make much sense to us today.

Long Tradition

Down the ages there have been various kinds of stage entertainment called pantomime. Two thousand years ago, the Romans enjoyed their *pantomimus*. This was performed in mime. A quite different kind of pantomime grew up in England during the eighteenth century, based upon some of the stock characters in the long-established Italian type of theatre called *Commedia dell'Arte* (see also page 33). One of these characters was Harlequin – whose name crops up in the pantomime shown here.

English pantomime was not especially comic at first, but became more so as time went by. There were pantomimes based on many themes or stories, often poking fun at monarchs and other rulers in the tradition of political satire.

It was only towards the end of Queen Victoria's long reign that pantomime became a special kind of Christmas entertainment, based on such fairy tales as 'Cinderella' and 'Puss in Boots'. This type of pantomime borrowed ideas and conventions from yet other kinds of theatre. The classic pantomime 'dame', such as Widow Twanky, was (and, of course, still is) played by a man – a convention going back to the days when women were not allowed on the stage.

Dick Whittington and other 'principal boy' roles, by contrast, were (and still are) played by women. The origin of this was probably a type of eighteenth-century play or opera that featured a woman disguised as a man as an ingredient of the plot. Altogether, our pantomimes are a real hotchpotch of theatrical ideas and traditions.

Rowdy Audiences

Victorian audiences could be pretty rowdy, to judge by the upper picture. Several members of this audience are giving the actors a piece of their mind! Three rows back it looks as if there's going to be a fight. Strong drink and other refreshments are in evidence. The lad with the cane and the girl with her shawl hanging over the balcony are exchanging very saucy glances, despite her boyfriend! We generally think of the Victorians as rather stuffy people. Perhaps we should think again!

Boating

There is a song called 'Messing about on the River'. These ladies and gentlemen at Henley Regatta in 1891 are certainly taking things nice and easy. All are dressed in fashionable summer clothes of the period. There is a lady wearing the type of straw hat called a 'boater', and a gentleman in a striped blazer. What was called a nigger minstrel band – very popular at the time – has come to serenade them.

Henley Regatta

Boating in the last century was almost exclusively a recreation for the well-to-do; and the Regatta at Henley-on-Thames was one of the big social events of the year. But it was by no means all as relaxed as this scene suggests. Regattas are mostly concerned with rowing, an activity that makes demands on nearly every muscle in the body.

There are two main categories of the sport. In what is actually called rowing, each member of a team, or oarsman, handles just one large oar. Such teams usually consist of eight oarsmen, plus a coxswain (cox for short), who directs the team effort and steers the boat. In sculling, by contrast, the oarsman handles two oars. He may scull on his own (single sculls), or with a partner (double sculls).

One of the oldest, established sports events anywhere is a sculling race on the Thames in London, traditionally held for young watermen who had just completed their apprenticeship. This dates from 1715. Henley Royal Regatta was started in 1839. This century it has attracted the best oarsmen from all over the world, and has been the venue for some very exciting Olympic events.

The first Oxford and Cambridge boat race was also held at Henley, in 1829 – several years before the regatta was thought of. The next of these famous university races did not take place until 1836, after which it became an annual event. For several years it was then raced on the Thames in London between Westminster and Putney; thereafter between Putney Bridge and Mortlake.

America's Cup

It is a long way from the quiet reaches of the Thames to sailing a yacht on the high seas. Yacht racing of a kind dates from the time of Charles II. In the last century, Cowes on the Isle of Wight was a world centre for yachtsmen. In 1851 the Royal Yacht Squadron offered a silver cup for a race round the island. This was won by an American schooner actually named *America*. Despite many challenges, the America's Cup, as it became known, was retained by America until 1983, when the Australians won it.

Opera

Our picture shows a big scene in Verdi's opera *Aida*. It is the story of a war between ancient Egypt and Ethiopia, in which an Egyptian soldier, Radames, falls in love with an Ethiopian slave girl, Aida, and betrays his country.

Monteverdi

The Latin word *opera* means 'the works'; and such a great feast of music and spectacle certainly is 'the works' in every respect. Opera did not start like that. It began in Renaissance Italy, when a group of noblemen became interested in ancient Greek drama. They believed this had originally been performed in a sort of sing-song voice. The man who made such entertainment into something really exciting was Claudio Monteverdi. He wrote truly dramatic music for the characters to sing, and added more drama by his clever use of instruments. This was all happening around the year 1600.

In the following century, opera became a sensation at the court of the French King Louis XIV at Versailles, where the singing was combined with spectacular ballet scenes (see also page 19). Then it became popular in London, thanks to George Frideric Handel. He wrote opera mainly in a style called *opera seria*, which drew upon Greek mythology and ancient history for its plots and scenarios. There was also *opera buffa*, or comic opera.

In *opera seria*, the singers were always first in importance. Wolfgang Amadeus Mozart wrote some of the most beautiful music of all for the voice, but his operas *The Marriage of Figaro* and *Don Giovanni* dealt with dramatic situations and human feelings in a deeper way than any written before him. Soon after, Ludwig van Beethoven in his opera *Fidelio* brought to the stage revolutionary ideas about liberty and justice. Opera became weightiest of all in the huge works of Richard Wagner. He wanted also to combine music, poetry and drama into a new super art form. Wagner's biggest achievement was *The Ring of the Nibelungs* – four separate but linked operas or 'music dramas' based on ideas and images from Norse mythology.

Verdi

Giuseppe Verdi lived at the same time as Wagner. He wrote some very grand operas, as we can see, but they are generally more tuneful and straightforward than Wagner's. In Italy, Verdi was followed by Giacomo Puccini, whose *La Bohème* and *Madame Butterfly* are full of lovely soaring melodies. Other well-loved operas are *Carmen* by Georges Bizet and *Eugene Onegin* by Peter Tchaikovsky.

Cycling

'You'd look sweet, upon the seat, of a bicycle made for two!' The words come from an English music-hall song, but they could have been specially written for this young French bride and groom, just off on their honeymoon in 1897. Behind them, half the other wedding guests have bicycles too. Cycling then was all the rage.

Penny Farthing

In the late eighteenth century there had been a craze for small coaches propelled by pedals. Then there appeared vehicles that looked like bicycles, but without any pedals. They were popularly known in England as 'hobby horses', since they were developed from a child's toy of that name. The rider had to stride along until his hobby horse gathered enough speed for him to raise his feet off the ground for a minute or two.

Cycling really got going, in about 1850, with the amazing 'Penny Farthing', so named because of its very large front wheel and very small rear one. Pedals were attached directly to the front wheel, which was made as large as possible in the interests of speed. Mounting one of these machines was an art in itself. The rider stood astride the little wheel at the back, while leaning forward to grasp the handlebars on top of the big front one. With a push to get the vehicle moving, he then heaved himself very quickly up on to the saddle, thence to go careering off, perched 2 metres (6.6 feet) high in the air. These perilous machines were not originally called Penny Farthings but *Ordinaries* – despite their extraordinary appearance.

By the 1890s, most bicycles and tricycles had a chain drive from pedals to a rear wheel, which led to much safer and more comfortable designs, and to a new cycling craze among women. Fashionable ladies in London, Paris and New York took to the roads in their thousands – at about the time the young couple in our picture were also setting out on their tandem. By riding their own bicycles and dressing as they pleased, these ladies were striking a blow for female emancipation.

After the First World War, cycling was very popular with both men and women, allowing thousands to tour the countryside on their holidays, at a time when most people did not own a car.

Cycle Racing

Cycle racing has been a popular sport ever since those reckless young men in caps and breeches hurtled along on their *Ordinaries*. Some events are held on circuits. There is also cycle-cross racing over rough country. Then there are the great road races, like the Tour de France.

The Circus

'Circus' is a Latin word meaning 'ring' or 'circle'; and in the days when Rome was the capital of a mighty empire, the *Circus Maximus* or 'Big Circle' (though it wasn't strictly that shape) was the most popular place of entertainment. It was used mainly for chariot racing, and for displays of wild animals.

According to contemporary accounts some charioteers also learnt balancing acts on horseback, like that shown in the picture opposite; while others tried to tame the animals and teach them to perform tricks. So there is a real link between the Roman *Circus Maximus* and the kind of circus we know today.

Blondin and Léotard

This is a unique blend of thrills, spectacle and fun, inspired by great artistes of the past. Take the high-wire and trapeze acts. In the last century two of the greatest exponents of these acts were Frenchmen. One was Blondin who, in 1860, crossed high over Niagara Falls on a wire, balancing on a pair of stilts and carrying another man on his back!

That same year Jules Léotard highlighted the skills of the circus trapeze artist when he appeared at London's Alhambra music-hall, flying high above the heads of the audience, with no safety net to catch him if he fell. A song was written about him, with the words, 'He flew through the air with the greatest of ease, That daring young man on the flying trapeze!' The special kind of one-piece vest and tights worn by circus high-fliers and acrobats is called a leotard after him.

Clowns

Then there are the clowns. In the picture we have one traditional type of clown with white face and Harlequin-style costume. The other type, with baggy clothes and elaborately made-up face, is known as an 'Auguste', or 'silly fool', and owes much to a great eighteenth-century theatre clown named Joseph Grimaldi.

In some countries circuses have permanent homes, almost like theatres. But in most countries, they are travelling shows, putting on their performances in a giant tent called the Big Top.

The United States was a great place for such circuses seventy or eighty years ago. Our picture is a poster for Barnum and Bailey's Circus, perhaps the most famous of them all. There was also Buffalo Bill's Wild West Show, which included real cowboys and Indians, and once played before Queen Victoria. The fabulous sharpshooter Annie Oakley appeared with him – the girl who inspired the stage and film musical *Annie Get Your Gun*.

Motor Sport

Here's a picture – a painting not a photograph – that captures the drama of motor racing in 1928. One Italian-built Bugatti overtakes another in the Rome Grand Prix. Note the crankshaft handles in the front, for starting the engine. The colour of the machines is important. Blue was the official motor-racing colour of France. Italy had red; while the British colour was dark green.

Paris to Peking Race

As early as 1895 there was a race from Paris to Bordeaux and back – a distance of 1,179 kilometres (732 miles) – that included steam and electric cars as well as petrol-engined ones. The winner completed the race in 2 days and 48 minutes. Next came races from Paris to Madrid, and then from Paris to Constantinople (Istanbul). In 1907 came the most stupendous of them all – Paris to Peking. The distance was some 14,000 kilometres (nearly 9,000 miles), with sections of the route so bad that cars had sometimes to be pushed, pulled, ferried over great rivers, and even carried across ravines. The winner finally made it in 60 days of epic motoring. Back in France, the first Grand Prix (literally Big Prize) race round a circuit was held in 1906 at Le Mans, now the venue of the famous 24-hour race.

Many enthusiasts consider the 1920s and 1930s to have been the golden age of motor sport. Italian Bugattis and Alfa Romeos, German Mercedes and Auto Unions, and British Bentleys, were all supreme for a few exciting years. During the same period, British drivers, including Henry Segrave, Malcolm Campbell and John Cobb, pushed up the world land speed record from 215 km/h (133 mph) to 591.7 km/h (369 mph). The official record today is 1,001 km/h (622 mph), held by a rocket-powered car.

Nine Million Cars

Just as colourful has been the story of private motoring. The first 'horseless carriages' were not taken kindly to by most people. They made a lot of noise, created poisonous fumes, frightened horses, and frequently crashed into things. In some countries they were only allowed to go at a walking pace, led by a man with a red flag. Drivers themselves, perched behind the wheel with no protection from the elements, wore goggles, scarves, and thick gloves.

Soon after the First World War, motoring developed into one of the world's biggest industries. By 1920, there were nine million cars in the USA, many of them made by that pioneer of mass production, Henry Ford. The way was open for the motorway, the multi-storey car park, the traffic jam ...

Jazz

Jazz bands like this were a common sight in New Orleans sixty or seventy years ago. The enormous brass instrument is a sousaphone, a kind of tuba specially designed for men to play on the march. It is named after John Philip Sousa, the American bandleader who wrote many famous marches.

New Orleans is the traditional home of jazz. It is a seaport near the mouth of the Mississippi river, and at one time handled most of America's cotton trade. The people who worked on the cotton plantations were black men and women, whose parents or grandparents had been shipped across the Atlantic from Africa as slaves. Their folk music (see also page 19) was based on African tribal dances and songs.

Beginning of Jazz

Several things happened to turn their music into jazz. President Lincoln abolished slavery in 1863, during the American Civil War. But the war itself ruined the cotton plantations, leaving thousands of black people jobless. Many then drifted to the cities, and especially to New Orleans. There they met the local Creole populations, people of mixed black, French or Spanish descent. The Creoles had attractive songs and dances of their own, which the new arrivals from the plantations soon learnt. Black people also acquired drums, trumpets, trombones and other instruments left behind by the old army bands at the end of the war.

The early jazz bands, dating from around 1890, played in dockside saloons and dance-halls, in street parades and funeral processions, and on the colourful Mississippi pleasure boats. They played the old 'blues' of the plantations, and the Creole-inspired dances called 'rags' and 'stomps'. Few of these early jazz bandsmen were trained musicians.

Jazz-style Dances

Within a few years, jazz was being played and heard everywhere. Black people themselves took it with them to other American cities, like St. Louis and Chicago. Such pioneer jazzmen as trumpeter Louis Armstrong, pianist and bandleader Ferdinand 'Jelly Roll' Morton and blues singer Ma Rainey made gramophone records. Jazz-style dances like the Charleston and Black Bottom became a craze in London and Paris. In these ways, jazz progressed from being the music of a relatively few black people to the new music of America, and then the new music of the whole world.

Jazz itself developed new forms and styles, such as boogie. Jazz led to swing and jive, and on to the pop-music revolution of the 1950s.

The Cinema

'This is another fine mess you've got me into!' groans poor Ollie as Stan backs the car through the garage wall. Stan Laurel and Oliver Hardy, the screen's most lovable pair, are as popular now as they were fifty years ago.

The First Cinema

The story of the cinema really begins way back in the eighteenth century, when people were thrilled by magic-lantern shows. Then came photography. As this improved, inventors looked for ways of taking rapid sequences of photographs, then projecting them at the same speed on to a screen, to create the illusion of motion. Louis and Auguste Lumière of France produced the first practical motion-picture camera and projector, which they called the *cinématographe*. In 1895 they opened the world's first 'cinema' in Paris.

Motion pictures, or films, were not taken seriously at first. They were novelties lasting a few minutes only, showing such things as trains arriving at a station. By 1910 more original films were being made, with real stories to them. France, Britain, Germany, Italy, Russia, all had a hand in their making. But it was half-way across the world, in Hollywood, California, that the new film industry grew fastest.

One of Hollywood's first directors and producers was Mack Sennett. Charlie Chaplin and Stan Laurel began their comic film careers at his Keystone studios after they arrived in the USA from England. Sennett also employed Buster Keaton, and created his own riotous Keystone Kops. Other directors were making serious films, such as D. W. Griffith, whose *The Birth of a Nation* about the American Civil War, is a landmark in the history of the cinema.

The 'Talkies'

These, of course, were all 'silent' movies, though they were usually accompanied by plenty of sound, ranging from an old piano in the local village hall to large electric organs with special sound effects in the big new 'picture palaces'. The first movie with its own sound track was *The Jazz Singer*, starring Al Jolson, made in 1927. A few years after 'the talkies', colour came to the screen.

In all these developments Hollywood led the way. Its stars became household names around the world. Then, just as the cinema had earlier ruined vaudeville and the music-hall, so in the 1950s television ruined Hollywood. Many of its big studios went out of business. Good films are still being made, but the days when going to the cinema was a way of life for millions have sadly passed away into history.

Concerts

The most famous series of concerts in the world today are The Proms. Their full name is the Henry Wood Promenade Concerts, because Sir Henry Wood organized and conducted them for many years, and because at one time the audience could stroll about during the performance. This photograph was taken at a Last Night of the Proms in London's Royal Albert Hall.

A Modern Orchestra

We are looking over the shoulders of the double-bass players, down towards the conductor. The other stringed instruments of the orchestra – violins, violas, cellos – are placed on either side of him. In the centre of the platform are the woodwind – flutes, clarinets, oboes, bassoons. Behind them, and coming closer to us again, are the brass – trumpets, horns, trombones, tuba. On the far side of the platform we can see the kettledrums and other percussion instruments, two harps and a piano. The orchestra also has a choir singing with it. What a contrast it makes with the group of medieval musicians on page 12.

Orchestras, as we think of them, did not begin to take shape until about 1600. The idea of an orchestra grew apace during the following century, when violins, violas and cellos, made by such master craftsmen as Antonio Stradivari, took the place of the older bowed, stringed instruments called viols.

Through the time of J. S. Bach and Handel (from about 1700 to 1750), orchestras grew in size and in the variety of instruments they included. But it was during the second half of the eighteenth century (known as the Classical period) that the kind of orchestra featured in our picture really began to take shape. This was a period when many royal courts had an orchestra attached to them.

Franz-Joseph Haydn was a court composer. He joined with others in making the orchestra a well-balanced group of instruments, demonstrating this in his many symphonies (then an exciting new type of music).

Conductors

After Haydn, nearly every famous composer wrote music for the orchestra. They also wrote music requiring more and more instruments, so that through the nineteenth century the orchestra grew from an ensemble of about thirty-five players to one of a hundred or more musicians. (How many can you count in this one?) This was when conductors became important. They were needed to organize rehearsals and direct orchestras in new music that was increasingly difficult to play.

Football

This picture shows Paolo Rossi of Italy (in blue) scoring a goal against West Germany in the 1982 World Cup final in Spain. This is association football or soccer – the only true 'football', we might say, since rugby football and American football permit the use of hands as well as feet. Throughout the world today, it is followed, in giant floodlit stadiums and on radio and television, by more people than any other sport or pastime.

Mob Football

A primitive form of the game, known as 'mob football', was played back in the Middle Ages, when crowds charged through narrow streets in pursuit of a ball, wrecking shops and injuring bystanders. Things got so bad that in England the game was banned in the year 1314.

It was in England that the modern game was launched in 1863, with the foundation of the Football Association (FA). This was followed in 1871 by the creation of the English FA Cup competition, and the formation of the Scottish Football Association in 1873. The game in those early years was strictly amateur; it was against the law for players to be paid for their skills. But by the time the Football League was established in 1888, professional footballers were allowed.

An interesting feature of the game itself in its early days was that it consisted mainly of running and dribbling with the ball. Passing the ball from player to player and tactical play came in only gradually. There were some very high scores in those early days too. In the Scottish FA Cup competition of 1885, Arbroath beat a club named Bon Accord by 36 goals to nil.

By the turn of the century, soccer football was spreading fast to other countries. Within Europe, the 'Fédération Internationale de Football Association' (FIFA) was formed in 1904, and quickly extended its authority round the world. Football was first included in the Olympic Games in 1908. The greatest of all competitions, the World Cup, was first staged in Uruguay in 1930.

World Cup

The prize to be won was the Jules Rimet Trophy, named after the Frenchman who was president of FIFA at the time. This was won outright by Brazil in 1970, after their third victory in the competition, and a new trophy, simply called the FIFA World Cup, is now played for.

Football has produced many star players. In Britain, one of the greatest was Bill 'Dixie' Dean, who scored a record 60 goals for Everton in 1928. The legendary Brazilian Pelé scored more than a thousand goals during his career.

Pop Music

Paul McCartney is one of the biggest names in pop music. Back in the 1960s, he and John Lennon wrote words and music to The Beatles' greatest hits. When that world-famous group broke up in 1970, Paul was very soon launched on a new career with his wife Linda and a new group called Wings. Here they are on stage, with Paul and Linda over on the right.

Rock-and-Roll

'Pop', of course, is short for 'popular'. But pop music has come to mean something much more than that. It began in the 1950s, when the big swing and dance bands, popular for so long, suddenly went out of fashion. In their place came small groups, or individuals, backed by guitars and drums. They played rock-and-roll, as different from the music of the dance bands as popcorn is from cream cake. The actual music – a pepped-up version of the old jazz boogie style (see page 49) – was not new.

What *was* new was the way it was performed. The clothes and manner of rock-and-roll stars expressed a whole new way of life. Elvis Presley, with his sulky looks and shaking hips ('Elvis the Pelvis'), influenced the life style of a generation of young people, perhaps more than any single person before him.

One thing that helped pop music enormously was electronics. The two really grew up hand in hand. Rock-and-rollers modified the tone of their guitars, and added to their volume (loudness), by connecting them up with loudspeakers. Then came synthesizers ('synthesis' means 'building up'), electronic miracles that created and mixed sounds in a way that had never before been possible. Recording studios could also add individual sound-tracks on top of one another, to achieve more amazing sound effects.

In discos, electronically-powered pop music pounds away at people's eardrums, stunning them into a state of forgetfulness. Pop groups, with such attractively odd names as 'Tangerine Dream', have used synthesizers and recording techniques to conjure up dream-like, psychedelic sound effects.

Offshoots

Some people think pop music all sounds the same. In fact, it has been growing and changing from the time the first rock-and-roller picked up his guitar. One early offshoot of pop music was called skiffle. Then there has been rock, hard rock, acid rock, soul, heavy metal, punk, reggae (a special type of music connected with the West Indian Rastafarian religious movement), to name but a few other offshoots.

Sources of Further Information

Music. For those interested in old or unusual musical instruments, here are some museums worth visiting: the Horniman Museum, London Road, Forest Hill, London SE23 3PQ; the Musical Museum, 368 High Street, Brentford (it has a fine collection of mechanical pianos and musical boxes); the Bagpipe Museum, St. Nicholas Street, Newcastle-upon-Tyne; the Russell Collection of Harpsichords and Clavichords, St. Cecilia's Hall, Niddry Street, Edinburgh. Two useful information books about music are *The Oxford Junior Companion to Music*, 2nd edition, edited by Michael Hurd (Oxford University Press) and *The New Encyclopedia of Music* by Alan Blackwood (Ward Lock). For jazz lovers, there is *The Illustrated Encyclopedia of Jazz* by Brian Case and Stan Britt (Salamander Books).

Opera. Worth reading are: *The Concise Oxford Dictionary of Opera*, 2nd edition, by Harold Rosenthal and John Warrack (Oxford University Press); *A Young Person's Guide to the Opera* by Helen Erickson (Macdonald & Co.); also *Enjoying Opera* by Noel Streatfeild (Dobson); and *The Performing World of the Singer* by Alan Blackwood (Hamish Hamilton), which is an introduction to the life and work of singers, from opera to pop.

Theatre. *The Oxford Companion to the Theatre*, 3rd edition, edited by Phyllis Hartnoll (Oxford University Press), has interesting features on pantomime, Punch and Judy shows and the *Commedia dell'Arte*, as well as many articles about great actors and actresses, plays and playwrights. Two other unusual books are *The History of the English Toy Theatre* and *A History of Punch and Judy*, both by George Speaight and published by Studio Vista. For those interested in a theatrical career, one helpful organization is the British Theatre Association, 9 Fitzroy Square, London W1. The Victoria and Albert Museum, Cromwell Road, London SW7, has a theatre museum which is well worth visiting.

The Cinema. For a very long and detailed history, there is *A History of the Cinema* by Eric Rhode (Allen Lane). A good general reference book is *Halliwell's Filmgoer's Guide*, 7th edition, by Leslie Halliwell (Granada Books). *The Cinema Greats* by Jeremy Pascall (Wayland) contains a biography of Laurel and Hardy; also worth reading is *Mr Laurel and Mr Hardy* by John McCabe (Robson Books). For keen students of the cinema, there is the National Film Archive at the British Film Institute, 81 Dean Street, London W1V 6AA. An appointment is needed to see its big collection of film stills, posters, etc.

Association Football. Footballing books and annuals are too numerous to mention. For detailed information about all aspects of the game, there is the Football Association, 16 Lancaster Gate, London W2 3LW. Most local clubs are also very helpful, especially to younger players.

Cricket. Perhaps the most detailed of the sport's many reference books is *Wisden's Cricketer's Almanack*, edited by John Woodcock. It is published annually, so as well as being full of information about games and individual performances, it is always up to date.

Motor Racing. Information on this sport can be obtained from the RAC Motor Sports Association, 31 Belgrave Square, London SW1X 8QH. For budding racing drivers, there is the Jim Russell International Racing Drivers' School, with bases at Snetterton Circuit, Norwich NR16 2JX, and at Silverstone Circuit, Towcester, Northants., NN12 8TL. The Donington Collection at Castle Donington, near Derby, is one of the world's best racing-car museums. The National Motor Museum at Beaulieu, Hants., has displays of vehicles from 1895 up to the present day.

Rowing. Information about this sport can be obtained from the Amateur Rowing Association, 6 Lower Mall, London W6 9DJ.

Cycling. Further information on this activity can be obtained from the British Cycling Federation, 16 Upper Woburn Place, London WC1.

Travel. Two interesting books on the growth and development of tourism are *Cook's Tours* (Blandford) and *Thomas Cook* (Wayland), both by Edmund Swinglehurst.

Horse-Racing. The National Horse-Racing Museum, 99 High Street, Newmarket, Suffolk, contains a lot of interesting information on the history of this sport. *Horse-Racing* by Peter Churchill (Blandford) is worth reading.

Glossary

Amateur: A person who plays a sport or takes part in something for enjoyment, and not for money, as a professional does.

Antiquities: Objects from ancient times, for example coins, statues, etc.

Blood sport: A sport involving the killing of an animal, for example hunting foxes.

Commedia dell'Arte: A type of unrehearsed comedy performed by groups of travelling players that emerged in Italy at the time of the Renaissance (see below), and flourished until the early eighteenth century.

Crest: A badge.

Crinoline: A framework of steel hoops worn beneath a petticoat or a skirt to make it stick out.

Crook: A pole with a hooked end used by shepherds.

Crusader: A person who went on one of the military campaigns in the eleventh, twelfth and thirteenth centuries to recapture the Holy Land from the Muslims.

Eisteddfod: A festival held in Wales which has competitions in music, poetry and dance.

Ensemble: A group of musicians.

Female emancipation: Freeing women from their traditional roles in life – primarily from being child-bearers and house-minders.

Hoarding: A screen of wooden boards on which adverts or posters are displayed.

Hotchpotch: A jumbled mixture.

Immortal: A person who is remembered for a long time after their death.

Marquee: A large tent.

Medieval: See *Middle Ages*, below; this is the adjective which describes the period of the Middle Ages.

Menagerie: A collection of caged wild animals.

Middle Ages: This can mean the period from the fourth to fourteenth centuries but usually, and in this book, it means the period from the eleventh to fifteenth centuries.

Mime: A play without any speech, in which actors tell the story by gestures and facial expressions.

Pagan: A person who does not belong to an accepted religion, like Christianity.

Pageantry: A colourful ceremony.

Pioneer: To do something or invent something before anyone else.

Provençal: Something connected with Provence, a region of southern France.

Prudent: To be careful and wise.

Regatta: A race or series of races for boats.

Renaissance: The period of European history marking the end of the Middle Ages and the start of the 'modern' world. It is usually considered as beginning in Italy in the fourteenth century.

Revolutionary: Bringing about great changes in ideas, etc.

Satire: A novel, play, film in which topical issues or personalities are made fun of.

Troupe: A group of actors, dancers, etc.

Vaudeville: A stage show with a lot of short acts – for example, comics, acrobats, magicians and dancers – popular in the early twentieth century.

Vice: A bad habit.

Acknowledgements and Sources of Pictures

page 10 Illustration taken from a medieval manuscript. (The British Museum)

page 12 Illustration taken from a medieval manuscript and hand-coloured for this book. (The British Museum)

page 14 Facsimile of a miniature from a manuscript in the *Bibl. de l'Arsenal*. (Wayland Picture Library)

page 18 Detail from a painting by the Flemish artist David Vinckebooms (1578–1629) entitled 'The Thames at Richmond, showing the old Royal Palace'. (Fitzwilliam Museum)

page 20 18th-century engraving by William Hogarth (1697–1764); hand-coloured for this book. (print Wayland Picture Library)

page 22 Painting entitled 'Southwark Fair', also by William Hogarth. (negative Wayland Picture Library)

page 24 Detail from painting by the 18th-century Italian artist Giovanni Antonio Canale (1697–1768), entitled 'Venice: the Basin of S. Marco on Ascension Day'. (The National Gallery)

page 26 Engraving taken from a book called *Old and New London*; hand-coloured for this book. (Wayland Picture Library)

page 28 Black-and-white drawing by M. S. Morgan for *The Illustrated London News* (1860); hand-coloured for this book. (The Illustrated London News)

page 30 Victorian jigsaw puzzle. (Wayland Picture Library)

page 32 Colour print of Punch and Judy; source and date unknown. (Mary Evans Picture Library)

page 34 Hand-coloured illustration taken from *Felix on the Bat* (1845). (Mary Evans Picture Library)

page 36 (top) An illustration by Fred Barnard from Richard Southern's book *The Victorian Theatre – A Pictorial Survey* (1970). (University of Bristol Theatre Collection)

page 36 (bottom) Another illustration from Richard Southern's book. (University of Bristol Theatre Collection)

page 38 Drawing from a journal dated 1891; hand-coloured for this book. (Wayland Picture Library)

page 42 Front-cover picture from the French newspaper *Le Petit Journal* for 28 March 1897. (Mary Evans Picture Library)

page 44 Colour printed poster *c.*1890. (Mary Evans Picture Library)

page 46 George Ham illustration (colour print) taken from *L'Illustration* of 1928. (Mary Evans Picture Library)

Photographs

page 16 The biennial game of chess being played with humans in Marostica, north-eastern Italy. (The Italian State Tourist Office)

page 40 *Aida* being performed at the Royal Opera House, Covent Garden. (Reg Wilson)

page 48 New Orleans jazz festival. (David Redfern)

page 50 Scene from an early Laurel and Hardy film. (National Film Archives)

page 52 Last night of the Proms. (BBC)

page 54 Italy scoring during the 1982 World Cup final. (All Sport/Steve Powell)

Index